CHEQUERS

STITIA
ENAX

CHEQUERS

The Country Home of Britain's Prime Ministers

Plantagenet Somerset Fry

London: Her Majesty's Stationery Office

Civil Service Department

First published 1977

Design: HMSO Graphic Design, Vera Brice
Photography: John Bethell

Front cover: An autumnal view of Chequers, from the south-east
Frontispiece: The south front of Chequers
Back cover: The doorway from the Forecourt to the rose garden was put in by Lord Lee in 1912

ISBN 0 11 630230 5

Contents

Foreword

by the Rt Hon. Lord Peart, Lord Privy Seal and Chairman of the Administrative Trustees of the Chequers Trust

Chequers is the official country residence of the Prime Minister. It was given to the nation by Lord Lee of Fareham, a remarkable statesman who aspired to, and achieved, high office in some of the administrations between 1903 and 1922. Lord Lee intended Chequers to be a private home for the use of Prime Ministers, and the Chequers Trust has carried out his wishes by keeping the estate free from intrusion. It is never open to the public.

In recent years it has been Government policy to reduce elements of mystery surrounding many aspects of national administration and to foster public interest in them; for instance, in Government buildings, Parliamentary and Departmental functions, Parliamentary proceedings and so forth. So, too, with Chequers, and the Trust has agreed that more should be revealed about the house and grounds. In wishing at the same time to preserve the privacy of the whole estate, the Trustees are asking for no more than any owner would reasonably demand for his property.

Lord Lee intended that Chequers should provide a peaceful and secluded environment in which Prime Ministers could rest before returning to work relaxed and refreshed. His hopes have been more than fulfilled. Every Prime Minister who has stayed at

Chequers during his years of office has come to regard it not as simply an official residence, but as a real home.

This book outlines the history of the Chequers estate and its owners since its inclusion in the great Domesday Survey nearly 900 years ago. It looks at the career of Lord Lee and it takes the reader inside the house, a charming Tudor mansion put up on the site of a much earlier building, to see the principal rooms and some of the works of art collected by Lord Lee and presented to the nation with the estate. It ends with some anecdotes about the various holders of the supreme office of Government who have occupied Chequers since Lloyd George moved in at the beginning of 1921.

The Lord Privy Seal of the day is always chairman of the Chequers Trust. He is also the Cabinet Minister who represents the interests of Her Majesty's Stationery Office. It is thus with doubled pleasure that I welcome this volume, written as it is by HMSO's first editor of books.

April 1977

Introduction

In 1917 Sir Arthur Lee, MP for Fareham and Director-General of Food Production, bequeathed his home, Chequers, near Wendover in Buckinghamshire, to the nation. It was to be the official country residence of the Prime Minister, after Lee and his wife died. Three years later, by now Lord Lee of Fareham, he advanced the date of the Prime Minister's occupation of the house by offering to move out at once, so that Lloyd George could begin to enjoy it there and then. Lloyd George spent his first week-end there as 'tenant-in-office', as it were, on 8th January 1921, and from that date, except in the time of Bonar Law (1922–3), the house has been used regularly by the Prime Minister of the day.

In his deed of settlement handing Chequers to the nation, Lee wrote a preface. Part of it read:

'It is not possible to foresee or foretell from what classes or conditions of life the future wielders of power in this country will be drawn. Some may be, as in the past, men of wealth and famous descent; some may belong to the world of trade and business; others may spring from the ranks of the manual toilers. To none of these in the midst of their strenuous and responsible labours could the spirit and anodyne of Chequers do anything but good. In the city-bred man especially, the periodic contact with the most typical rural life would create and preserve a just sense of proportion between the claims of town and country. To the revolutionary statesman the antiquity and calm tenacity of

Chequers and its annals might suggest some saving virtues in the continuity of English history and exercise a check upon too hasty upheavals, whilst even the most reactionary could scarcely be insensible to the spirit of human freedom which permeates the countryside of Hampden, Burke and Milton.

Apart from these more subtle influences, the better the health of our rulers the more sanely will they rule, and the inducement to spend two days a week in the high and pure air of the Chiltern hills and woods will, it is hoped, benefit the nation as well as its chosen leaders. The main features of this scheme are therefore designed not merely to make Chequers available as the official country residence of the Prime Minister of the day, but to tempt him to visit it regularly and to make it possible for him to live there, even though his income should be limited to his salary'.

Lord Lee clearly intended Chequers to be a private place of rest for the Prime Minister – a second home, it is true – but nonetheless a place wherein to throw off the cares of state, to unwind and by taking advantage of the Chiltern air to revitalize himself. Anxious to ensure that it should not be a museum – or even look or feel like one – Lee arranged the furnishings so that they might be what one would expect to find in any like house in the British countryside.

Chequers is something of a mystery to most people, not surprisingly, for it is not open to the public. When the news is given out that the Prime Minister is entertaining a visiting head of state or is to hold an important meeting at Chequers, they wonder where and what it is. Some think of it as an official house somewhere in the country, not far from London – they are not exactly sure where. Perhaps it is an imposing and formal building like No. 10, Downing Street, only shut away in a wood. (In fact it is readily visible from the road and there is practically nothing formal about it.) Some have even confused it with Chartwell, the home of the late Sir Winston Churchill. They really do not know. Nor do they know about the man who gave it to the nation and how the gift came about. This book is a brief answer to those puzzles.

It would not have been possible to write about Chequers without consulting the authoritative and readable account of its history and architecture written by the late J. Gilbert Jenkins (*Chequers: a History of the Prime Minister's Buckinghamshire Home*, Pergamon Press, 1967). D. H. Elletson's *Chequers and the Prime Ministers* (Robert Hale, 1970), gives a full account, with numerous anecdotes, of the Prime Ministers who occupied Chequers from 1921 to 1970. Lord Lee printed ten copies of his own papers in 1939 for circulation to friends, under the title *A Good Innings: The Private Papers of Viscount Lee of Fareham*, PC, GCB, GCSI, GBE, and these were edited by Alan Clark and published by John Murray, in 1974. They reveal more about the man than anything else so far published. And Lord Lee contributed a memoir to the *Catalogue of the Principal Works of Art at Chequers*, put together by the Victoria and Albert Museum and published by HMSO in 1923. In addition to these primary works, memoirs and biographies of the Prime Ministers and the leading personalities with whom they worked abound, and these have been consulted.

I owe a debt for much help and encouragement to Lord Shepherd, Lord Privy Seal and Chairman of the Chequers Trust from 1974 to September 1976, and to Lord Peart, his successor in both rôles. Wing Commander Vera Thomas, Curator at Chequers, has been extremely helpful to me and to HMSO Graphic Design staff, for which we are grateful. Above all I want to record my sincere appreciation of the invaluable help and counsel given unstintingly by Group Captain J. M. Ayre, secretary of the Chequers Trust.

Plantagenet Somerset Fry

1

The first nine centuries

Chequers has almost 900 years of recorded history. It is included in Domesday Book (1086), that remarkable inventory of England's properties and their contents which lists everything down to each pig and cow, as an estate of 14½ hides (about 1250 acres) held by Maigno the Breton in Ellesborough in Buckinghamshire. Nearly half a century later it was in the hands of an Exchequer official, Elias de Scaccario. Scaccarium was the Latin for chequer-board and Exchequer accounts were settled on a chequer-board table. The Norman-French version of de Scaccario was de Chekers, or del Checker, and this is the origin of the name of the estate.

Elias died in the reign of the Lion Heart, Richard I (1189–99), and his son Henry inherited the interest and enjoyed it for half a century. Henry was something of a property speculator, and he acquired considerable lands elsewhere in Buckinghamshire and also in Berkshire. He attracted the notice of Henry III (1216–72) who knighted him, and he died in the 1240s, leaving the estate to his second son Ralf de Scaccario. Ralf was probably the first member of the family to use the name de Chekers. He died in 1254, leaving no son to follow, and the estate, with whatever buildings were on it, passed jointly to his daughters Agnes and Catherine.

There is some doubt about who occupied Chequers for the generation or so after Ralf's death, but by the last years of the 13th century Catherine had married William de Alta Ripa, of Algarkirk in

Opposite. The hill with the clump of trees (at left) is Beacon Hill, 756 ft high with commanding views over many counties. In his Deed of Settlement giving Chequers to the nation, Lord Lee reserved the right to be buried on Beacon Hill, but as it turned out he was interred at Avening in Gloucestershire, where he died.

The arms of the Hawtrey family set in the alabaster headpiece of the Great Hall chimneypiece.

Lincolnshire, they had had children, including a son, William, and they were firmly in possession of the estate. The name Alta Ripa was changed to the Norman-French Haut Rive which in time became Hawtrey. Chequers remained in the Hawtrey family for more than 300 years, until 1597, when William Hawtrey (1518–97) died without male heir. In the middle of the 16th century Hawtrey rebuilt the house, finishing the work in 1565, and that house is substantially what can be seen to-day.

It is interesting to divert a little attention to William Hawtrey, the first person of any real prominence to own Chequers. He lived for 79 years, nearly double the average span of Elizabethan men. He gave more than half a century of service of one kind and another to the state, to local affairs and to the business community. He was twice sheriff of Buckinghamshire (the first time, of Bedfordshire as well). He was a JP and member of Parliament for Buckinghamshire in the 1562–3 Parliament, while in the reign of Mary I (1553–8) he had been employed in an Exchequer post (like his predecessor at Chequers, Elias de Scaccario). Hawtrey became an original member and shareholder of the Muscovy Company of London, founded in 1555 to promote trade with Russia, and was still a member 20 years later. But his most dramatic service to the state was in 1565 when William Cecil, on behalf of Elizabeth I (1558–1603) and her Privy Council, ordered him to provide protective custody at Chequers for Lady Mary Grey, sister of the Lady Jane Grey who had been executed in 1554 by Mary I following the abortive attempt of the Duke of Northumberland to install her as queen on the death of Edward VI. Clearly Cecil, always one to pick the right man for the job, regarded Hawtrey as a trustworthy gaoler.

Lady Mary Grey had broken one of the cardinal rules of the Elizabethan Court–she had married without the Queen's permission. Worse, Lady Mary had married beneath her in social terms, for while she was cousin of the Queen – and indeed a possible

Hans Eworth's portrait of Lady Mary Grey, painted in 1571.
Panel, $16\frac{1}{2}$ ins × 12 ins.
Lord Lee acquired it in 1922 and presented it to Chequers.

heir to the throne–her husband, Thomas Keyes, was but a sergeant porter to the Royal Household. The fact that Keyes was over six feet tall and Lady Mary diminutive, almost a dwarf, and the resulting derision that this ludicrous contrast provoked, must have offended Elizabeth who was not one to suffer jokes at the expense of members of the royal family. Keyes was sent to Fleet prison in London, and Lady Mary was condemned to the care of Hawtrey at Chequers, whose instructions were quite explicit: '. . . You shall not suffer her to have any talk or commerce with any stranger that shall come or send to her otherwise than yourself or your wife shall be privé unto . . . neither shall she go out of your house above, except it be necessary for her to take the ayre for her health, for Her Majesty would have her straightly used from enjoyning of any liberty, as a means to correct her . . .'

Lady Mary spent two years locked up in what is called the Prison Room (p.36), which was a room on the top floor of the mansion, reached by a tiny spiral staircase secreted in one wall. She was released in 1567 but kept apart from her husband who died soon after he was freed from Fleet prison.

Hawtrey married three times, but while each match brought him additions to the family wealth, they did not in the end give him a surviving male heir to inherit Chequers. His only son, William, knighted by Robert Devereux, Earl of Essex, in 1591, was killed at the siege of Rouen a few weeks later. William Hawtrey the elder arranged for his son's eldest daughter, Mary, aged about 12, to be married by special licence to Francis, only son of Sir John Wolley, Latin secretary to Elizabeth I. The Chequers estate was settled on the couple who, when they reached adulthood, drifted apart. Francis died in 1609 and Mary spent the rest of her life at Chequers, dying in 1637. The estate passed to her sister Brigetta, wife of Sir Henry Croke, MP, the son of Sir John Croke, Speaker of the House of Commons in the last years of Elizabeth I.

Brigetta Croke died scarcely a year later, and the estate went to her husband. He buried her in the parish church at Ellesborough and put up a splendid monument which included in the inscription *Feminae nihil habens nisi sexum* (There was nothing feminine about her save her sex). Commonly thought to mean that she was something of a female dragon, the remark is actually a tribute, for it was a great compliment to women in those times to compare them with men. The Crokes retained Chequers for forty or so years, but it was only one of several properties in their ownership, and when Sir Henry's son, Robert, died in 1681, his daughter Mary inherited it.

She married John Thurbarne, MP for Sandwich and Serjeant-at-Law, but died without heir. The house went out of the family to his daughter Joanna by his first marriage who, when she came to Chequers, was the wife of John Russell, grandson of Oliver Cromwell, Lord Protector of England, Scotland and Ireland (1653–8) who is widely regarded as one of the greatest statesmen and rulers of all British history.

Chequers remained in the possession of the descendants of Cromwell, right up to Delaval Frankland-Russell-Astley who was killed in an air crash in 1912. In the early 1900s he had leased it to tenants. The last and most important of these were Arthur Lee, MP for Fareham, and his wife Ruth.

The link with the Cromwell family is marked at Chequers by the collection of Cromwell relics brought there by Joanna Russell and others, including Lee who had obtained some on the open market. It is fascinating that for over two centuries the house should have had these associations with the family of the Lord Protector, the chief executive of state, and then in this century have become the country home of the prime minister, also the chief executive of state. Nor can the similarities between the rôles of Cromwell and Churchill (in his first term as prime minister, 1940–5) go unnoticed. Prime ministers are first among equals in the govern-

The last of the Hawtreys to own Chequers, Brigetta Croke, grand-daughter of William Hawtrey. Painted, *c.*1620, by Marcus Gheeraerts the Younger.
Canvas, 73 ins × 43 ins.

ment, but Churchill, during the Second World War, had necessarily to wield powers hardly less absolute than those of Cromwell, though, as he was quick to explain, his dominating rôle could be brought to an immediate and permanent end by one adverse vote in the House of Commons.

The owners of Chequers, from Joanna Russell to the last of the Astleys, were not remarkable people. A succession of lawyers was kept busy as a stream of relatives, close and not so close, one after the other inherited and passed on the property. One occupant, Charles Russell, who fought with George II–the last English king to lead his troops into battle–at Dettingen in 1743, wrote several letters while he was away campaigning, in which he dwelt at length upon his longing for '. . . dear, delightful sweet Chequers where nought but peace, tranquillity and happiness can reign'. Nearly a century later the property was put up for sale. One young prospective buyer was Benjamin Disraeli, and in a letter to his agent he wrote: 'We . . . wish to purchase. I should suppose not under £40,000, perhaps £10,000 more, as there is timber; but at any rate I should like to leave half the purchase money on mortgage if practicable; if not, we must manage some other way.' The proposal went no further and in 1847 Disraeli, who was eventually to become Prime Minister, bought Hughenden, a few miles away.

No sooner had Lee obtained the life tenancy than, with the agreement of the last Astley, he decided to transform it. When, later on, he obtained the freehold, he gave it to the nation to be a country home for Britain's Prime Ministers. Its subsequent history has understandably been more eventful and dramatic than that of the eight centuries or so between its beginnings and the year 1909. Chequers appealed instantly to Lee and his wife who both lay awake half the night after being taken round it, working out how they might afford to lease it and restore it. 'The outside was as beautiful as we had been led to expect,' Lee wrote, 'but the interior was incredibly ugly; an orgy of Victorian Gothic and quite perversely inconvenient in its planning and appointments. Moreover, it could only be put right at such an immense cost that it seemed out of the question for us.' But by the next morning Lee had roughed out a scheme under which they could afford it if the Astleys would lease it to them for their lives, with a free hand over the restoration. Later on, Lee noted in his memoirs their excitement at the 'acquisition at last being clinched and contracts exchanged. We were now provided with an ideal home for the rest of our natural lives.'

Lee and his wife devoted a great deal of time, thought and money to restoring and improving the house. They consulted many experts, they visited well-known houses to study their interiors, and they searched far and wide for furniture, pictures, glass, porcelain, metalwork, carpets and other treasures to add to those already there, which had been accumulated over the centuries. The result was not a museum but a representation, as Lee put it, of 'what an old English house may contain which has been owned and cherished for many hundreds of years by people of taste and moderate means, who loved it as their home and who adorned it for their own gratification and comfort.'

That, in a nutshell, is the story of the Chequers estate and its ownership, up to the time of the Lees. Some of its owners adored it and, like Charles Russell, wrote lovingly of its tranquillity. Lee felt the same, and this has been echoed by most of its occupants ever since.

Who was this man that gave Chequers to the nation and what was the nature of the gift?

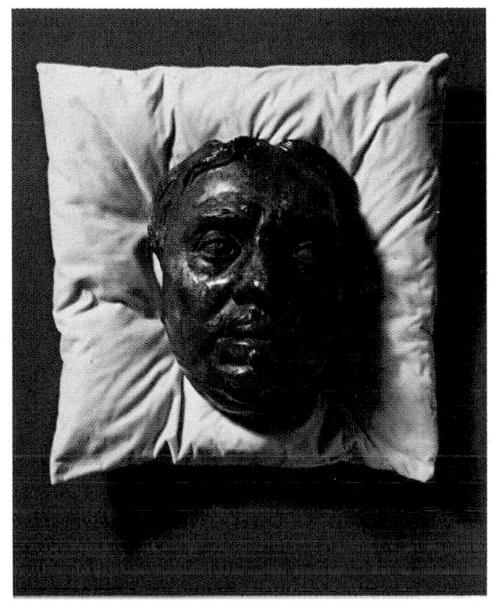

What was believed to be a life mask of Cromwell but is now thought to be a cast from a bust of the Lord Protector by Edward Pierce (1635–95), made, probably, several years after Cromwell's death in 1658.

Opposite. The three-quarter length portrait of Oliver Cromwell by Robert Walker who was described by Gilbert Jenkins as the court painter to the Commonwealth.
Canvas, 49 ins × 39 ins.

Opposite. Frances Cromwell, the Lord Protector's fourth daughter, by H. Van Der Myn.
Canvas, 48 ins × 38½ ins.
Frances married, 2ndly, Sir John Russell, 4th Bart., and their son John married Joanna Rivett (*nee* Thurbarne), heiress of Chequers.

2

A man of strong personality

Arthur Hamilton Lee was the son of a Dorset rector and grandson of the sailor Sir Theophilus Lee, who served with Nelson at the Battle of the Nile. His father died in 1870 when Lee was only two and he grew up in considerable poverty with a mean and dominating guardian on whom he was foisted by his mother.[1] This up bringing helped to mould him into a blunt and uncompromising individual. His unrequited need for affection made him want very much to be liked, something that motivated many of his actions throughout his long career. He also developed a certain naivity that explains his unpredictability, which often disconcerted his colleagues.

Through natural aptitude and sheer hard work Lee won a scholarship to Cheltenham College, and from there he went to the Royal Military Academy at Woolwich. He was commissioned in the 'Gunners' and posted to Hong Kong. During his service there he organized an unofficial reconnaissance of the defences of the Russian port of Vladivostock, which earned him the praise of the Commander-in-Chief, the Duke of Cambridge. Less complimentary, however, were the reactions of Lord Salisbury, the Foreign Secretary, who virtually threatened he would repudiate him if this kind of thing happened again.[2]

1 *A Good Innings: the Private Papers of Viscount Lee of Fareham,* edited by Alan Clark, John Murray, 1974, pp.9–19. 2 ibid, p.39.

Opposite. Looking across the rose garden on the south side of the house.

Lee returned to England to a post in the Isle of Wight and there he met and made friends with the ageing Poet Laureate, Lord Tennyson. In 1893 Lee was sent to Canada as lecturer in military history at the Royal Military College at Kingston in Ontario. While in Canada he joined the famous Klondyke Gold Rush of 1896 as a reporter for the *Daily Chronicle*.

In the Spanish-American War of 1898–9, he served as British military attaché with the American forces. His frankness struck a sympathetic chord with the tough American leaders, in particular with Theodore Roosevelt who became and remained a close friend for the rest of his life. Lee displayed great gallantry on several occasions in the Cuban campaign and his exploits were fulsomely praised by the US Commander, General Miles, in a letter to Field Marshal Viscount Wolseley, Commander-in-Chief of the British Army. The British War Office responded to this by promoting him lieutenant-colonel and appointing him British military attaché at the embassy in Washington. Before he left for England Lee had met and fallen in love with Ruth Moore, elder daughter of a very wealthy New York banker.

Lee returned to the US and married Ruth Moore. This transformed his life. The wealth she and her sister Faith had inherited from their father was such that Lee need never work again if he did not want to. And in the fulness of time it enabled him to make the magnificent gift of Chequers to the nation and to endow it.

In 1900 Lee came back to England with his bride, gave up the army and stood for Parliament. In the 'Khaki' election he won the seat at Fareham in Hampshire as a Conservative, and entered the Commons on the same day as Bonar Law and Winston Churchill. He was well equipped to embark upon political life and all that it entailed. He bought the lease on No. 10, Chesterfield Street, in Mayfair, and also the lease on Rookesbury Park, Wickham, near Fareham. He also bought a new car, a 12-horse-power air-cooled

Lanchester. And soon his career advanced. He made his mark in the House by his forceful manner of speaking, often startling and sometimes alarming the Tory Party by his independence of the strict party line. When Balfour and Chamberlain threatened to split over Tariff Reform, Lee joined the latter, but Balfour, wanting his talents nevertheless, in 1903, appointed him Civil Lord of the Admiralty. 'My foot was really on the ladder at last', Lee wrote.

The hectic years of ministerial office–and of active opposition after the Conservatives were defeated in 1905–with the concomitant and ceaseless social round, taxed his strength, and he and his wife decided to leave what they felt was the enervating climate of Hampshire and seek more vigorous air. This is how they came to Chequers in 1909.

We have seen that the Lees fell in love with Chequers practically at first sight. To begin with, they envisaged it as a home for themselves for their lives, for it was only as life tenants that they had moved in. Then, in 1912, Delaval Astley, the last owner of Chequers, was killed in a flying accident. The property passed to his widow who had not liked it much and regarded it only as a possible source of funds. The Lees saw this as an opportunity to acquire the estate as their own freehold and it was soon after that the idea of giving the house to the nation was supposed to have been born. This is substantiated by Gilbert Jenkins who records that, according to Bonar Law, the intention to hand over the house was formed as early as 1912.[1]

It took nearly five years for the Lees to obtain the freehold, however, and this long interval has not been explained. But finally on 6th April 1917 the legal documents were signed. Lee's wife, and her sister Faith Moore who lived at Chequers with them, decided to provide the necessary money jointly as a present to Lee so that he

1 Parliamentary Debates, Vol. c. 936.

Lord Lee (as Arthur Hamilton Lee, MP) by P. A. de Laszlo, which the artist presented to Lady Lee (then Mrs Lee).

Lady Lee of Fareham, by
P. A. de Laszlo

could carry out his wish to present Chequers to the nation as sole owner. Lee wrote to Lloyd George, then Prime Minister, formally offering the house to be the country home of Britain's first minister, after the death of Lee and his wife. On 29th August Lloyd George replied, accepting the gift and offering in addition to be chairman of the trustees who were to administer it. But this is to anticipate.

In the years between 1909 and 1917, Lee's career had taken several strides. He had actively supported the campaign to get more Dreadnought battleships built and is credited with having coined the catch phrase 'We want eight and we won't wait'. He entertained Theodore Roosevelt at Chequers for several days when the latter came to Britain on an official visit in 1910. Meanwhile, Lee continued to expand his political associations in order to win support for this advancement. To some extent, however, his abilities, although considerable, were blunted by a frankness which sometimes led to indiscretion, and an unwillingness to compromise. In an environment where such qualities were less acceptable than they are now, it is not surprising that he did not always find a welcome in those circles in which he most wanted it.

When the First World War broke out in 1914, Lee, who was then 45, rejoined the army. He was made a colonel and held several staff appointments. Chequers was temporarily turned into a military hospital. In October 1915 he came back to England, having earned the gratitude of the great War Minister, Lord Kitchener, and having won two mentions in despatches in the battlefield. He left the army to resume politics and was appointed parliamentary secretary to Lloyd George who had just become Minister of Munitions. In this crucial rôle Lee proved to be an outstanding administrator.

Although he was still a Conservative MP, Lee began to fall under the spell of the radical Lloyd George – as did so many others – and he gave Lloyd George the most devoted service. When Lord Kitchener was tragically drowned in HMS *Hampshire* in June 1916,

Lloyd George moved to the War Office and took Lee with him as his personal military secretary. A few weeks later Lee was created a KCB in the Civil Division.

This closeness with Lloyd George did not go unnoticed among Tory party managers and supporters, particularly among those with landed interests, and they were not to overlook it. The time was to come when they would exact their revenge.

Colonel A. H. Lee, as Liaison Officer, G.H.Q. in France, 1915.

In December 1916 Asquith was ousted, Lloyd George formed a government and at once took over the direction of the national war effort. He was, however, Prime Minister of a coalition of parties and he could not fill all his ministries with friends. Bonar Law as Conservative leader blocked any appointment for Lee for several weeks, chiefly on personal grounds, but by February Lloyd George had found him a niche, making him Director-General of Food Production in the Board of Agriculture. It was a rôle that demanded immediate action and swift results – the production of more food for a population that was being deprived of it through the successful German submarine campaign against shipping.

Lee's energy and drive did a great deal to prevent an acute food shortage. Exhorting – and where possible compelling – landowners to put to the plough areas hitherto reserved for pasture or recreation (putting and bowling greens, lawns and even cricket pitches were not always spared), he set a good example at Chequers by ploughing up practically all the land there, except for the woods, and seeding it. But there was bound to be a confrontation with Tory landed interests, and he handled it less sensitively than they would have liked.[1] In the summer of 1918, when the need for such draconian production policies had passed, the Tories took their revenge. They obstructed his Food Production Programme, which would have put another million acres of grassland under the plough, to the point where he felt compelled to offer to resign in protest – as they hoped. Lloyd George, however, felt that Lee might do better to fight these interests in the House of Lords and offered him a peerage. Lee accepted on condition he was given the necessary 'teeth' to carry through some if not all of his programme.[2] He chose the title Lord Lee of Fareham.

In 1919, despite strenuous opposition by Bonar Law, Lloyd

1 *A Good Innings*, edited by Alan Clark, p.167. 2 ibid, pp.177–180.

George appointed Lee Minister of Agriculture, with a seat in his 'Peace' Cabinet. Lee brought to the job the same high administrative abilities, but also the same frankness and reluctance to compromise, and he records in his papers something of the stormy times of his tenure of office. In 1921 Lloyd George moved Lee to the Admiralty. It was to be an unpopular job because the Government had reluctantly decided to truncate the strength of the armed services, and the Prime Minister believed Lee was the right man to get the Sea Lords to accept drastic cuts in naval expenditure. Lee's wife, Ruth, noted in her diary that the Admiralty had been his principal ambition for many years, and there is no doubt about the singularly adroit manner in which he undertook the rôle.

Something of his tendency to take the independent line manifested itself during the Washington Naval Conference in 1921, set up to limit naval construction among the great powers. The British

Some of the delegates at the Washington Conference on limitation of armaments, 1921. In the right-hand corner of the centre square of tables are: Arthur Balfour (left) Lord Lee and Sir Auckland Geddes (right).

delegation was led by A. J. Balfour, with Lee as a member. During the visit Lee made a speech advocating the end of all submarine construction. He had not forgotten that his task as Director of Food Production during the war had been to make up the deficiencies in food supplies which were brought about by the German U-boat campaign against food-carrying convoys to Britain. He had, moreover, been disgusted by what he felt was a hypocritical stand by the French delegation who were widely believed to be covering up the fact that France was actively expanding its submarine building. Balfour was embarrassed, naturally, but when *The Times* attacked Lee, the Sea Lords, led by Admiral of the Fleet Earl Beatty, rallied to his support.

The next year, Lloyd George's coalition collapsed and Lee was one of many ministers who lost office. For him it was the end of his political career. By this time, however, he had already handed over Chequers permanently to the nation and the first of the Prime Ministers had begun to enjoy it.

Lloyd George had accepted in principle the generous offer of the Lees in August 1917. The story was given to the press soon afterwards and it occupied several lead columns in most national and provincial papers. Reaction to the scheme was mixed. Lee's friends applauded the gesture and editorial opinion on the whole supported it. But Lee expected opposition and criticism, and he records it in his papers. Nonetheless, it was by any standards an imaginative and munificent scheme and one for which all Prime Ministers since 1921 (except for Bonar Law who declined to take advantage of it) have had good reason to be grateful.

A deed of settlement formally transferring the property to the nation was executed on 24th November 1917 and in it Lee set out the objects of the gift, the wording of which is recorded in the Introduction. A sum of money was transferred to the Public Trustee to form the Chequers Trust Fund whose income was to be used for purposes such as wages for servants, upkeep of the gardens, repairs and maintenance to the building and so forth. But the deed had to be incorporated in an act of Parliament, and in December the Chequers Estate Bill was passed by the Commons without amendment.

The Lees stayed at Chequers for the next three years, but then decided to bring forward the date of handing it over to the Prime Minister. They left the house for good in January 1921 and moved into White Lodge at Richmond. From that moment Chequers became what it is today, the country home of Britain's Prime Ministers.

Lee's subsequent career after the fall of Lloyd George's government, when he was advanced from a barony to a viscountcy, is one of public service mingled with private pursuits, notably in the picture collecting field, the former gradually giving way to the latter. He was Chairman of the Royal Commission on the Indian Civil Service (1923–4) for which he received the highest India Office honour, a Knight Grand Commander of the Star of India (GCSI). He chaired other Royal Commissions. His title and his experience got him a number of City directorships which for a time filled the gap. But as he faded out of public life, he devoted more and more of his energies into building up a second and more ambitious collection of pictures 'with zest and rare flair for finding and acquiring masterpieces of all schools and dates' (*Dictionary of National Biography*). He left the collection in his will to the Courtauld Institute of Art at London University, which he and Samuel Courtauld had founded. He was also a Trustee of the National Gallery for some years.

In the 1930s Lee and his wife moved to their last home, a quiet country house in Gloucestershire and there, in 1947, he died.

3

A perfect country house

There is nothing outstanding about the house or its architecture, but it is a very pleasing, medium-sized Tudor mansion, a good example of the kind of comfortable building put up in that age when the leading men of the kingdom rose to the top through political skill or business acumen and not through accident of birth or prowess in war. It stands in a sheltered hollow some 630 feet above sea level, 'upon a plateau of the Chiltern hills' (to quote one of the Astleys), surrounded by a lovely park of slopes and spurs, here and there thickly wooded with beech and box, larch and holly. It is the perfect setting for a house in the country, a house where men at the centre of affairs can for a while revitalize themselves.

Some of the parkland lies much higher than the house. From Beacon Hill, which rises at the north-west to some 750 feet (named, possibly, after Hawtrey's heraldic device, a beacon set on fire) and from Coombe Hill, to the north-east, 100 feet higher still, you can, on a clear day, get the most marvellous views over the countryside, as far as Salisbury Plain and the Cotswolds. In the park there are many walks, taking one through the charmingly named Happy Valley, across Velvet Lawn, and up Cymbeline's Mount (a mount on which the ancient British King, Cunobelinus, is said to have built a fort).

The roads and tracks, dignified and unobtrusive, have their own

Opposite. The bay window at the west end of the Long Gallery. The 24 painted glass panels record the principal owners of Chequers from the de Scaccario (de Chekers) family in the 12th and 13th centuries to the Frankland-Russell-Astleys of the 19th and 20th centuries. They were commissioned by Lord Lee.

especial features. The drive from Great Kimble Lodge on the Princes Risborough road rises steeply through a wood of box trees,[1] whose size and growth put them among the most remarkable in England. The main drive, from a pair of lodges and gates built by Lee on the Great Missenden Road, runs northwards right to the semi-circle of lawn in front of the south side of the house. It is a development of the ancient approach to Chequers, and much of the work was done by German prisoners during the First World War. It was named the Victory Drive. Perhaps more appropriately, it was flanked in the 1960s by an avenue of beech trees presented by Sir Winston and Lady Churchill after they left at the end of his second term as prime minister, in 1955, 'in memory', as the plaque inside the front entrance reads, 'of the momentous days they spent

Opposite. Looking up the Victory Drive towards the south front. The beech trees lining the drive were presented to Chequers by Sir Winston and Lady Churchill.

Above. The north front.

1 Chequers is one of the very few places in Britain where box is indigenous.

The South Front of Chequers, as it is today.

at Chequers from 1940–1945 and 1951–1955'.

The house is built of local brick whose colour has mellowed into a gentle warm pink-red that is brought out by the light grey stone in the string courses, the gable copings and the window mullions. Some of this stone is replacement work done at the beginning of this century and is a faithful reproduction of the remaining stone-work of the Tudor period. Part of the north front of the house is thought to incorporate the remnants of a 15th-century building on the site, but Hawtrey's reconstruction was a thorough one and

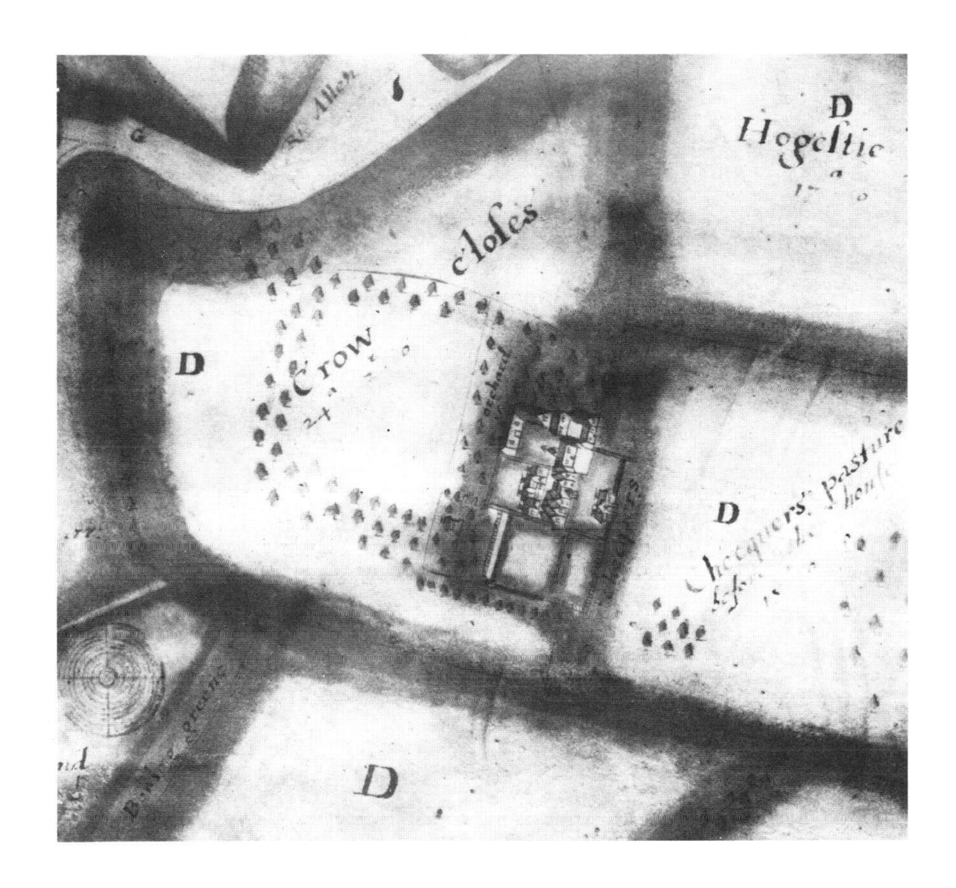

Part of a large map of the Chequers estate, drawn in 1629. The section reproduced here shows the house as it then was.

even the north wall was substantially rebuilt, to feature two large double-storeyed bays with parapets. In the facing of the eastern parapet is a panel bearing the Hawtrey arms, and the 'beacon' device with the initials WH and AH and the date 1565.

The south front is interesting. The two end gables of equal height are Hawtrey-built. The higher extension at the west end was added by Sir Robert Frankland-Russell in the mid-19th century. The central bay was erected sometime after Hawtrey's death but possibly before 1629, to judge from an estate map of Chequers of that year which has survived. On this map there appear five gables in the south front. At some time there had been an entrance through the front into a courtyard between south and north fronts, a yard that was open until about a century ago when it was roofed over. At the end of the last century, during the stone replacement works, the Astley family motto *Justitiae Tenax* was set in concrete letters on either side of the central bay, at first-floor level, and it can be seen today from some distance.

On the south side of the house, where the original forecourt and approach had been, Lee, with the advice of Avray Tipping, the well-known landscape gardener, built the South Garden, with its garden houses. It was laid out in the formal Elizabethan manner and sheltered by buttressed brick walls to the south and west. The main entrance to the house is now to the east of the mansion, through a new porch in the Tudor style, also built by Lee. To enhance the approach he put up new gates and had a new Forecourt designed round a quatrefoil-shaped lawn, in the centre of which stands a statue of the Goddess of Health, Hygeia, partially overshadowed by what was once one of the finest tulip trees in England.

It is probable that the inside of the house received as many different kinds of treatment over the years as the outside. Lee, whose trenchant comments on the interior are quoted earlier (p. 7), set out to reconstruct it as thoroughly as possible in the Elizabethan style, but without damaging too much of the original. He consulted the distinguished architect Sir Reginald Blomfield and over the next years wrought a wonderful transformation. The major improvements were to the Great Hall, the Hawtrey Room, the Stone Hall, the Dining Room, the Great Parlour and the Long Gallery. But every part of the house felt the touch of restoration in some way or other.

The Stone Hall is the first room reached when you have gone in

Opposite. The Forecourt leading to the main entrance to the house. The Tudor style porch was added by Lord Lee who also found and sited the statue of Hygeia in the quatrefoil-shaped lawn.

The Stone Hall. The opening at left
leads to the Great Hall and main staircase.

The Hawtrey Room.

through the Lee porch. It is beautifully panelled in stripped and bleached oak. Just below the ceiling on the wall facing you is a balustraded opening to light the staircase behind. On the right there is a moulded stone doorway, part of the Hawtrey reconstruction, and this was uncovered by workmen when chipping away mountains of Victorian Gothic plaster. Hawtrey had put his initials in wax into the spandrels of the arched doorway which leads into the Hawtrey Room. This was the main room of the house for centuries. The bay window facing north contains in its topmost lights eight heraldic panels of stained glass, associated with the Hawtrey family. The Hawtrey Room was L-shaped, but the short arm of the 'L' has been partitioned to make a small parlour. In this part there is the door, forming part of the wall panelling, that leads to the tiny spiral staircase which used to take one up to the Prison Room at the top of the house.

Another archway from the Stone Hall leads to the Great Hall. This central room used to be the open courtyard. When it was roofed over in the 1870s, it was embellished with a hideous carved oak gallery which, with a palm tree in a pot in the centre of the room, made the whole area resemble the lounge of a Victorian hotel on the south coast which had seen better days. Blomfield took all that out, put in a new ceiling which was an exact copy of one re-erected as an exhibit in the Victoria & Albert Museum, erected a Palladian arcaded screen with a galleried passage along the first floor leading to bedrooms, and installed a huge alabaster chimneypiece whose front panel contains three coats of arms, the families of de Chekers, Hawtrey and Lee. One wall is largely filled with a huge mullioned window looking out on to a small yard, the remains of the older open courtyard. Blomfield also inserted at first-floor level, opposite this, a fine 16th-century mullioned window that Lee had found in a house being demolished in Ipswich. It lights the staircase up to the first floor.

The Dining Room looks out to the south and is L-shaped. When Lee took the house the Hawtrey Room was the dining room, but it was over 100 feet away from the kitchen (on the other side of the Great Hall). Servants had to carry all the food either across the Great Hall, which was also the main living room, or 'to dive down a steep flight of stairs into the cellar, cross the cellar and ascend into the dining room by a service staircase at its north-west corner'. Meals must have been stone cold. Lee converted the old kitchen and scullery into a new dining room and put in the gloriously rich 17th-century oak panelling.

On the first floor major improvements were made to the Great Parlour and the Long Gallery. The Great Parlour is above the Hawtrey Room, and is the same size. The fine panelling, inlaid with holly and bog oak and supposedly made by Dutch refugees driven out of the Low Countries during the occupation by Spain in the late 16th century, was bought by Lee from a house at Ipswich, which may have been the same one from which the mullioned window in the Great Hall came. Dominated by a splendid long mahogany dining table, with several leaves, and surrounded by heavy carver chairs, the Great Parlour now has much more the air of a conference chamber than of the living room it used to be.

The Great Parlour opens into the Long Gallery which takes up the greater part of the first floor on the north front. This is the most magnificent room in the house, lined almost all round with bookshelves, most of them put up by the Russells two centuries ago. It is light, colourful, warm and relaxing. At the west end a bay window has 24 panels of painted glass depicting the arms of the owners of Chequers from Elias de Scaccario to Bertram Astley, all reconstructed at Lee's initiative. The book collection and the other treasures housed in this room are outlined later (pp. 51–4) but it may be apposite to mention here that among them is the ring worn by Elizabeth I and conveyed by Sir Robert Carey on her death

These two views illustrate the main features of Lee's reconstruction of the Great Hall. At right in the lefthand picture is part of the mullioned window looking out over the small courtyard. Over the mantelpiece, in the righthand picture, is the Lely picture, The Perryer Family.

Before 1870, the Great Hall and the smaller courtyard had been one yard open to the elements.

The Dining Room

up the length of England to James VI of Scotland in Edinburgh to signify that he had succeeded as James I of England, too. There is also the much-quoted letter of Cromwell, written from the battlefield of Marston Moor, in 1644, in which he says that 'God made them as stubble to our swords'. And there are a despatch case and table used by Napoleon.

The Long Gallery was used by Churchill frequently during the Second World War as a cinema for relaxation after days or weeks of nerve-tensing work. One film he would see time and time again was 'Lady Hamilton', starring the young Laurence Olivier (now Lord Olivier), and as he watched he may have reflected upon the presence in a cabinet in that room of Nelson's own watch, another of the Chequers treasures.

Two other parts of the house are worth mention – the Prison Room and the Cromwell Passage. The Prison Room is a small attic

The Great Parlour.

The White Parlour is a small room facing south and is behind the arcaded screen in the Great Hall. In Lord Lee's time it was Lady Lee's favourite sitting room. The walnut long case clock, decorated in marquetry of various woods, was made locally by John Hill of Risborough, a few miles away.

Opposite. The most magnificent room in the house, the Long Gallery contains the library and many of the treasures and relics (p.51–4). On top of the mantelpiece can just be seen the two swords which were thought to have belonged to Cromwell. But like Robin Hood's slippers, Cromwell swords appear all over the country and any authenticity is impossible to prove.

bedroom above the Great Parlour. This is where Lady Mary Grey was confined for two years, and she left behind something of her sadness in Latin writing on the wall (now protected by glass). The garret was reached by the tiny staircase which spiralled inside the wall past the Great Parlour (with a door into that room) down to the Hawtrey Room. The Prison Room contains the portrait of her painted in her lifetime by Hans Eworth, found by Lee and presented to Chequers in 1922. The Lees spent the last nights of their time at Chequers in this room while the house was being prepared for the occupation by Lloyd George; they had slept in the same room 11 years before when they first moved into Chequers.

The Cromwell Passage – narrow but with a bay window – is connected to the Long Gallery. It has pictures of Cromwell and members of his family. In the bay stands – ironically – a handsome leather-covered brass-mounted chest which belonged to James,

Duke of York (later James II), son of Charles I whose trial and execution were brought about by Cromwell and others in 1648–9. In the window are several stained glass panels, one of which is a cluster of fragments bearing the inscription *Glass found from Houses of Parliament, German Air Raid, 10 May 1941*.

These are the leading features of the Chequers interior. The Lees furnished the rooms with great care for comfort, elegance and taste. They found numerous pictures, objets d'art, items of porcelain, silver, metalwork, carpets, rugs and clocks, to add to those things left behind by earlier owners, and they assembled them with long-thought-out attention to harmonious blending inside a well-planned reconstruction. But because the house was given to others to use, men and women whose tastes would certainly not be the same, and perhaps through natural wear and tear, the assemblage of contents is not as it was when the Lees left.

Opposite. The Prison Room, where Lady Mary Grey, sister of Lady Jane Grey, was confined for two years (1565–7) in the custody of William Hawtrey. The small painting at top right is the Hans Eworth portrait of Lady Mary Grey.

Opposite the Walker three-quarter length portrait of Oliver Cromwell (left) in the Cromwell Passage stands the brass-mounted leather-covered chest which is said to have been used by James II (1685–88) when he was Duke of York and Lord High Admiral. On the centre of the lid is an oval medallion bearing the badge of the Admiralty, an anchor with rope and cross keys. The chest is Restoration period, and its stand is early 18th century.
H. 3 ft 6 ins, W. 4 ft 2 ins, and D. 2 ft 4 ins.

4

Treasures of a collector

In his introduction to the official catalogue of the Chequers works of art (*A Catalogue of the Principal Works of Art at Chequers,* HMSO, 1923), Lord Lee emphasized that Chequers was not a museum. The furnishings and decorative objects he and his wife had chosen were but a demonstration that art is not incompatible with domestic comfort. The contents were intended to represent the tastes and collecting enthusiasms of generations of past owners, and on the whole they do that very well. If the choice of furniture is here and there a trifle pedestrian and the porcelain and pottery lacking in variety and colour, the picture collection has a much sounder and more imaginative touch, for by the outbreak of the First World War Lee had become something of an art expert. He was rapidly building up a collection of pictures that was regarded with some respect in the art world. This reputation was to grow, and after he had given Chequers to the nation and moved out of it, he started collecting again.

The catalogue lists nearly 900 items, embracing pictures, miniatures, prints and drawings, furniture, clocks, glass, stained glass, pottery, porcelain, goldsmiths' and silversmiths' work, metalwork, armour, manuscripts, autograph letters, tapestries, rugs, carpets, and miscellaneous relics of great historical figures like Cromwell, Nelson and Napoleon. In addition there are several hundred books

Opposite. The figure of Charles I dominates the scene in this English Delftware charger. The Prince of Wales (later Charles II) is at left, and the Duke of York (later James II) at right is holding a bird. Under the shield of his cloak is one of the king's daughters.

Sir Robert Walpole, KG, later first Earl of Orford (1676–1745), first Prime Minister of Great Britain, by J. B. Van Loo.
Canvas, 50 ins × 40 ins.

This portrait was given to Chequers by Lord Lee who also gave a smaller, half-length version of it to No. 10, Downing Street.

and maps, ranging from the 15th century down to Lee's own collection, augmented with volumes presented by Prime Ministers and others.

PICTURES

There are nearly 200 pictures at Chequers. They span three and a half centuries of painting, representing many Western European schools and including several works by masters. Some of the pictures were from the original collection of Oliver Cromwell, and reached Chequers through his daughter Frances. Other owners, both earlier and later, added to the collection. But the major contribution was made by Lee.

No one can say which is the best picture, but one that deserves consideration is *The Mathematician*, once attributed to Rembrandt. Lee bought it in 1911, but he does not say in his papers what it cost him. It came from the Ashburnham Collection and was known as the Ashburnham Rembrandt. It had been copied as a mezzotint engraving (a print of which Lee had also obtained) by James MacArdell in the 1740s and Lee was and remained convinced he had bought a genuine Rembrandt. Doubts have, however, been raised about its authenticity, and it is now attributed to the Dutch artist G. van den Eeckhout.

Many of the other paintings by leading artists of the 16th, 17th and 18th centuries are of considerable interest. After he had left Chequers, Lee found and bought the portrait of Lady Mary Grey painted by Hans Eworth in 1571, four years after she was released from her custody with Hawtrey and a year after her husband's death. Something of her melancholy is reflected in this picture. Lee gave it to Chequers in 1922. It is one of the oldest pictures in the house. Even older is the portrait of Margaret Beaufort, mother of Henry VII and great-great-grand-daughter of Edward III, which

The unfinished self-portrait by Sir Joshua Reynolds PRA (1723–92). It was formerly in the collection of the Marquise de Thomond.
Canvas, 19 ins × 23¾ ins.

Dedham Vale, by John Constable
RA (1776–1837), dated 5th
September 1821.
Canvas, $14\frac{1}{2}$ ins × 22 ins.

was painted by an unknown artist of the English School in about 1500.

One of Lee's purchases was the last portrait by Reynolds. A self-portrait, it was found unfinished on an easel in his studio after his death. Another was a pair of portraits by George Morland, better known as a painter of rustic scenes and country subjects. Lee also bought several pictures by Constable, including one of Dedham Vale. He contributed a woodland landscape by Gainsborough, *Landscape with Oak Trees* by John Crome, and a portrait of Dr Andrew Wood (physician to Sir Walter Scott) by Raeburn.

The collection boasts two Lelys, one of the Perryer family (described by Professor E. Waterhouse as a picture of five gloomy people who appear to be waiting for the end of the world in the presence of an over-lifesize bust) and the other of Edward Hyde, 1st Earl of Clarendon, Charles II's Lord Chancellor. There is a Kneller portrait of the great Duke of Marlborough, a picture of Princess Mary, Charles I's daughter, by Honthorst, and a portrait of Jacob Wilkinson (a Governor of the East India Company) by Zoffany, believed to have been painted in Calcutta.

Brigetta Croke, Hawtrey's grand-daughter and owner of Chequers from 1637–8, and her husband Sir Henry, were both painted by Mark Gheerarts the Younger and these pictures are at Chequers. Gheerarts was the painter of the well-known 'Ditchley' portrait of Elizabeth I, in 1592, which is now in the National Portrait Gallery. There is a fascinating link here. Ditchley was the Oxfordshire home of Sir Henry Lee, Elizabeth's Master of the Ordnance, and when she visited him there in 1592 she was painted by Mark Gheerarts, of whom Lee was an early and important patron. Three and a half centuries later, during the Second World War, Ronald Tree, then owner of Ditchley, put the house at the disposal of Winston Churchill for those weekends when the moon was full and Chequers was in danger of air attack.

William Hawtrey, who rebuilt Chequers in the 1560s. This miniature on vellum on card is by an unknown artist, but in the manner of Nicholas Hilliard.
H. $3\frac{1}{16}$ *ins, W.* $2\frac{9}{16}$ *ins.*

Another Chequers miniature, this is of John Pym (1584–1643), one of the leaders of the Parliamentary Party at the time of the Civil War. It is by Samuel Cooper, signed 'S.C.' in gilt on the dark brown background (at right).
H. $2\frac{3}{4}$ ins, W. $2\frac{3}{16}$ ins.

The Cromwell collection includes pictures of members of the Lord Protector's family by Robert Walker, who could be described as court painter to the Commonwealth. There is also an original Walker portrait of Cromwell. The collection has a number of miniatures of the Cromwells, mostly following the famous Samuel Cooper originals, and a Cooper miniature of John Pym, one of the greatest of the Parliamentary leaders, who died in 1643.

FURNITURE, CLOCKS, CERAMICS

Much of the furniture at Chequers is sound, well-made 17th- and 18th-century English, principally in oak or walnut. It is representative of the best craftsmanship of the times. No pieces are actually attributable to any leading cabinet-maker, but one suite of sofa and armchairs, made for Lady Russell, whose husband Sir John owned Chequers in the late 18th century, is in the manner of Hepplewhite.

There is a cabinet-on-stand which has great local interest. Of yellowish elm wood and in mid-17th-century style, it was made of wood from a tree not far from the house, known as King Stephen's Elm. This tree is believed to have been planted during the reign of Stephen (1135–54), that period of unremitting civil war and misery described by the Anglo-Saxon Chronicle as one of 'nineteen long winters'. After a century of use the cabinet was consigned to a garden shed where it acted out the rôle of seed store for forty or so years. In the 1830s it was rescued and given to an Aylesbury cabinet-maker to restore, and he used fresh wood from other trees on the estate to repair it. On a piece of the old veneer lying in a drawer is inscribed a run-down of the cabinet's history, which states that the elm tree was 27 ft in circumference. When it was blown down in a gale in 1890, the circumference was measured again and this time found to be 32 ft 10 ins. The stump was removed, but there are some promising suckers growing from its base.

The late 17th century elmwood cabinet on stand made from King Stephen's elm tree which stood outside the south east corner of the rose garden. Some of the wood was so hard that it blunted the edges of the tools used to restore the cabinet, in 1838. The convex front panel in the cornice is the front of a long drawer.
H. 5 ft 1 in, W. 3 ft 10 ins, D. 1 ft 8 ins.

Chequers has several cabinets-on-stands. This is a Chinese scarlet and cream lacquer cabinet on giltwood stand. The upper part has folding doors, decorated in tones of gold and scarlet with pagoda buildings, figures and landscapes with flowering plants, birds and insects, which enclose eight small drawers with a cream ground and similar decoration. The stand is probably Dutch, made in the second half of the 17th century.
H. 5 ft 2 ins, W. 3 ft.

The English furniture is well-balanced by a sprinkling of Western European pieces, notably chests and cabinets-on-stands. The oldest chest is 15th-century German, with iron mounts. One early 17th-century Flemish ebony cabinet, on gilt stand of later date, is said to have belonged to Cromwell.

There are five long-case clocks, and one of these, in marquetry-decorated walnut, of the 17th century, was made locally by John Hill of Risborough. It may have been made for the then owner of Chequers.

The porcelain and pottery at Chequers are predominantly the 'blue-and-white' style of which so much was made and is still collected with enthusiasm today. Some of it is Chinese, including examples of Ming, Chia Ching, K'ang Hsi and Ch'ien Lung. It is interesting to note that Lee, who put so much English-made furniture into the house, seems not to have cared much for English porcelain or pottery. There is, however, a fine 18th-century blue 'Chinese fisherman' pattern Caughley tea service, some Lowestoft, Worcester and Lambeth pieces, and perhaps the most famous piece of all, the English Delftware charger showing Charles I and his children.

AUTOGRAPH MANUSCRIPTS

The handwriting and signatures of famous people from the past are always fascinating, and at Chequers there is a collection of letters and manuscripts. There are bound volumes of letters signed by Napoleon, by his first wife Josephine, by other members of his family and by some of his marshals. Most of his letters are from the early part of his career, between 1796 and 1798. There are two Nelson letters written to Earl Spencer, First Lord of the Admiralty. And there are two by Cromwell, one of which has already been mentioned (p. 34).

whoe is already soe many wayes obliged to serve
your interest as well the Kings as your Eminence
may thinke this a fittinge way to witnesse that
satisfaction wch you have receaved in the successe
of his Negotiation, and to recompense him for his
care and fidelitye therein besids I have observed
that such as have formerly governed in theise
Nations have made the like requests wth very
good successe none of which have wished better
to Ffrance or had a more perticular affection
for your interest then my selfe and I assure
your Eminence the regard you shall have to my
recomendation in the disposall of this place upon
this person wilbe receaved by mee as a great
token of your freindship toward mee, and lay
a great obligation upon

Decbr. ye 4th
1657

Yr affectionate freind
Oliver P.

Part of a letter from Cromwell to Cardinal Mazarin in 1657, one of the Cromwell relics at Chequers. Jules Mazarin (1602–1661) was chief minister to Louis XIV from 1643 to his death. Successor to the great Cardinal Richelieu, Mazarin was one of the most influential statesmen in Europe. He had very great respect for Cromwell, and this was reciprocated.

Other manuscripts include a note from Richard Cromwell to Cardinal Mazarin in France about his father's death (September 1658), a letter from Louis XIII of France to his mother referring to Cardinal Richelieu's visit to her, a letter from Charles I to Louis XIII, and another from Ferdinand V of Spain to his daughter in 1483. There are letters written by Samuel Johnson, William Pitt, Edmund Burke, Warren Hastings, Lord Palmerston, Benjamin Disraeli, Robert Browning and George Meredith. Tennyson, whom Lee knew in the last months of the poet's life, is represented by a collection of letters and verses including an exchange between him and Walt Whitman.

RELICS

Every great house has an accumulation of famous relics. The Chequers collection has Napoleon's despatch case, the writing

During his career as the greatest naval commander of all time, Horatio Nelson received many gold watches. This one at Chequers was made by William Moore in London and the outer case bears Nelson's arms as Viscount Nelson, Duke of Bronte.
Diameter $1\frac{1}{2}$ ins.

table he used in exile on St. Helena, the key to the room in the house at Ajaccio in Corsica where he was born in 1769, the ring worn by Elizabeth I[1], Nelson's gold pocket-watch made by William Moore and inscribed with his arms as Viscount Nelson and Duke of Bronte, the octagonal watch with brass mounts said to have belonged to Cromwell's wife, Elizabeth, and what was thought to be a life-mask of Cromwell[2] discovered by Lee in a sealed wall cupboard. The two swords in the Long Gallery, said to have belonged to Cromwell, must however be suspected, as similar claims are made for like weapons in numerous parts of the country.

BOOKS

Some, though by no means all, of the owners of Chequers have taken an active interest in the library in the Long Gallery. While its 15th- and 16th-century books cannot be shown to have come there through Hawtrey, later owners such as Croke and Thurbarne did much to expand the range of books, and the 18th-century Russells brought in many continental works of great interest. Then, for over a century, little seems to have been added, until Lee's tenancy.

The two 15th-century books are an illuminated manuscript Missal from Bressanone, in the Tyrol, which, still in its original velvet binding, is a great rarity, and the first edition of Albertus Magnus's *Paradisus Animae*, printed in Cologne in about 1473, three years before Caxton first brought printing to England. The

1 The ring was given by James to the first Earl of Home, ancestor of Sir Alec Douglas-Home, prime minister and occupier of Chequers, 1963–4.

2 But Mr. Jenkins says that scholars have argued whether it is a life or a death mask and now think it is neither. It is suggested it was a posthumous study or a cast from a bust of Cromwell of 1672, taken from the wax funeral effigy, of which there is a plaster version in Florence.

Opposite. Queen Elizabeth I's ring. Made of mother-of-pearl, the shoulder is set with ten rubies. The bezel bears the monogram ER, (E in diamonds, R in blue enamel). Its lower part is set with ten rubies and a pearl and it opens to reveal enamelled portraits of Elizabeth and her mother Ann Boleyn *below*. Beneath the bezel is an oval medallion of a phoenix rising from a flaming crown, the Boleyn badge.

The open volume among these books from the Library in the Long Gallery is William Painter's *The Palace of Pleasure*, published in 1566, the source of the plot for Shakespeare's *Romeo and Juliet*.

Among the treasures at Chequers is a glass case containing six toy figures, Golliwogg and friends. These toys inspired the American children's writer Florence Upton to write a series of children's books on the adventures of Two Dutch Dolls and Golliwogg. The picture shows Golliwogg and one of the dolls.

early 16th-century books include the Aldine edition of the 18 Euripedes' tragedies (Venice, 1503), a first edition of Aristophanes' *Lysistrata* and *Thermophoriazusae* (Florence, 1513) and Lucian of Samosata's *Saturnalia*, translated by Erasmus and published in Basle in 1521 in a binding with the arms of Louis XIV of France.

The 16th- and 17th-century English books of importance are an early edition of Chaucer (William Bonham, *c.* 1545), first editions of Drayton's *Polyolbion* (*c.* 1613), Ben Jonson's *Workes*, Hobbes' *Leviathan*, Sir Thomas Browne's *Urne-Buriall* and Dryden's *Cleomenes*, the fourth folio of Shakespeare and the first illustrated *Paradise Lost* (1688).

Most important of all, however, is William Painter's *The Palace of Pleasure*, 1566. This is the first collection of short stories in the English language and it supplied Shakespeare with the plot for *Romeo and Juliet* and Webster that for *The Duchess of Malfi*. Only seven copies are known to exist, one of which is in the British Library.

The European books are mostly 18th century and are notable for their illustrations. These include La Fontaine's *Fables* (1755–9) with plates after Oudry, the Ibarra *Sallust* (1772), considered the finest example of Spanish book production of the 18th century, Manoel Carlos de Andrade's *Nobre arte de cavallaria*, with a fine series of plates of horsemanship, and a splendid set of Piranesi engravings including a copy of the *Veduti di Roma*.

Lord Lee collected stained glass. This German roundel, painted *en grisaille* and in yellow stain, dates from about 1550.
Diameter, 9$\frac{3}{4}$ ins.

5

Prime Ministers at Chequers

'My Dear Lee,

Your offer in regard to the Chequers Estate is most generous and beneficent, and one for which the Prime Ministers of England in the future will have much to thank you. The gift which you are now bequeathing in advance to the nation is on its very essence an indication of the practical thoughtfulness which is characteristic of you; and the public spirit which the scheme displays is worthy of that which its originator has shown in all my dealings with him. Future generations of Prime Ministers will think with gratitude of the impulse which has thus prompted you so generously to place this beautiful mansion at their disposal. I have no doubt that such a retreat will do much to alleviate the cares of state which they will inherit along with it, and you will earn the grateful thanks of those whose privilege it is to enjoy it.'

This was the first paragraph of a letter from Lloyd George, of 29th August, 1917, in which he wrote to Lee to accept his formal offer of Chequers to the nation. Three and a half years later, in January 1921, at a dinner party in the house, Lee and his wife handed Lloyd George the keys, so to speak, and left for London. As he went out of the main door, Lee hesitated, turned to Lloyd George and squeezed his arm, 'Look after it!' And from that moment, despite the comment Lloyd George made that Chequers was 'full of

Opposite. A view from the South terrace across the Park.

the ghosts of dull people', he did make use of the house, care for it and enjoy what it had to offer. For this we have the testimony not only of many friends but also of his two daughters, Olwen and Megan. When she heard that her father was going to resign (in October 1922), Megan could think of nothing else to say except 'Damn! There goes Chequers!'

During his twenty months at Chequers Lloyd George invited a great variety of people to stay for weekends and for meetings at other times. Apart from his Government colleagues and parliamentary friends of all parties, he entertained foreign guests, such as M. Briand, the French Prime Minister, Marshal Foch, and the Crown Prince of Japan who was so short in height that Lloyd George's grandchildren refused to curtsey to him and kept calling him 'The Prince of Pan'. Once, during a serious coalminers' strike, he invited the union leaders, Herbert Smith and others, to make use of the quiet of the house to hack out a settlement, and the idea of the visit was applauded by the press. Lloyd George even invited Lord and Lady Lee who declined because they dreaded the homesickness that would ensue. And it was at Chequers that the first meeting was held which led to the end of the Coalition and the close of Lloyd George's active career in government.

In September 1922, Lloyd George called a meeting of his Coalition ministers to discuss whether they should go to the country in a general election straightaway or not. The Chanak crisis was at its height and war with Turkey seemed unavoidable. The ministers agreed to ride out the emergency first and then go to the country. But it was not for the Chequers gathering to decide after all, for at another meeting, this time at the Carlton Club in London and this time of Conservatives only, the majority present voted to break up the Coalition and fight the next election alone. Lloyd George was beaten and he knew it. He resigned, went to the country, and lost disastrously, though of course he won his own seat yet again. He

David Lloyd George, OM, later Earl Lloyd George of Dwyfor (1863–1945), Prime Minister, 1916–22.

was out of office and it proved to be forever. Soon afterwards, Lloyd George left Chequers, and only returned once more about twenty years later, as a guest of Winston Churchill during the Second World War. One of his last official acts was to write to Lord Lee at the beginning of November to say that the King (George V) had approved of his recommendation that Lee should be advanced to a viscountcy.

Lloyd George was followed by Bonar Law, but 'that meekly ambitious man' (as Asquith once described him) declined to use Chequers at all. He hated the countryside – Lady Lee said he disliked anything that was beautiful – and he was strongly averse to Lee. So, under the terms of the gift, the chancellor of the exchequer, the next in line in the government entitled to use the house, moved in. He was Stanley Baldwin.

Baldwin liked Chequers enormously. On and off for fourteen years, first as Chancellor and then as Prime Minister for three terms[1], he spent a great many weekends there. Well known to the public as a country-lover ('To me, England is the country and the country is England,' he often said) he allowed the local hunt to meet there, umpired the cricket matches and involved himself in a variety of local events.

Baldwin's first ministry fell in the election of February 1924 and Ramsay MacDonald became Britain's first Labour Prime Minister. For the next 13 years he and Baldwin 'played Box and Cox in the matter of the premiership'[2], for his government lasted less than a year and by Christmas Stanley Baldwin was back at Chequers again. Five years later, the Conservatives were defeated and MacDonald returned to power – and to Chequers for weekends. In 1935 Baldwin was returned for his last ministry and he retired in 1937, accepting an earldom and handing over to Neville Chamberlain.

Ramsay MacDonald reacted to Chequers in much the same way as the Lees had in 1909, but while he loved the house and its historical associations, the practical man in him was stirred by the park and the gardens where he found plenty to do, often wielding a scythe or an axe himself. When he left at the end of his first short ministry, he wrote in the Chequers Visitors Book 'Farewell to this house of comforting and regenerating rest.' MacDonald had to

1 1923–4: 1924–9: and 1935–7.

2 Gilbert Jenkins.

Stanley Baldwin, later Earl Baldwin of Bewdley, KG (1867–1947). Prime Minister, 1923–4, 1924–9, 1935–7, at Chequers in 1924.

endure a lot of fun-poking at his role as a country squire. His Lord Chancellor, Lord Haldane, took it more seriously and complained that it was impossible to get hold of him when he was at Chequers.[1]

When MacDonald became Premier again in 1929, Britain was feeling its share of the Great Depression. There were difficulties

1 In a speech in the Lords, Haldane had attacked the principle of Prime Ministers having a week-end retreat at the time Lee made his gift, in 1917. He thought they ought to be available seven days a week in London, during Parliamentary sessions at least.

James Ramsay MacDonald, (1866–1937), Prime Minister, 1924 and 1929–35, with his daughter Ishbel at their home in Lossiemouth.

enough, but the lack of an absolute majority in the Commons meant tailoring much of the Labour programme to fit the acute economic conditions. MacDonald began to tire easily. He was already over 60 and had aged beyond those years. He turned to the solace of Chequers frequently, and in his case, at all events, Lee's words about the health of Prime Ministers benefiting from the pure Chiltern air rang sharply true. He made the first radio broadcast from Chequers in 1929. He entertained the first German official visitors, who included Chancellor von Bruening and the German Ambassador, von Neurath, who was to hitch his fortunes to the Hitler star and land in the Nuremburg dock in 1945.

Baldwin returned in 1935 and he, too, had aged prematurely. He found himself needing more and more the anodyne of Chequers, particularly during the two major crises of his term of office, the storm following the Hoare-Laval agreement that gave Italy Ethiopian territory as the price of European peace, and the abdication of Edward VIII.

To Neville Chamberlain, second son of Joseph Chamberlain, Chequers was an adventure into territory he barely knew – the country life. Despite his age – and he was nearly 68 when he first went to Chequers as Prime Minister, in 1937 – Chamberlain was remarkably fit. In the early days the week-ending in the Buckinghamshire air, in which he frequently walked several miles at a stretch, invigorated him still further. But the Munich crisis of the autumn of 1938 was enough to break anyone, and he began to show the strain swiftly and alarmingly. This was patently clear in the film shots taken of his return to England, waving the piece of paper which he really believed spelled 'Peace in our time'.

When Hitler ignored Chamberlain's ultimatum of 2nd September 1939, Chamberlain had perforce to declare war the next day. He was already a broken man. He, too, sought the tranquillity of Chequers, weekend after weekend, as if to lift himself out of the horrendous world about him. He was forced to resign the leadership of the government and before the end of 1940 he had died.

Winston Churchill took over the government in May 1940 and directed the national war effort for the next five years. He called up the spirit of the people of Britain and moulded it into a tough, uncompromising national determination not to yield to Hitlerite ambition and brutality. He transformed everything within his reach that had any direct bearing upon the prosecution of the war, and this included Chequers which became, according to Gilbert Jenkins, a power-house of strategy. Many meetings affecting the war in all its theatres were held there, and the major decisions that resulted were born and crystallized round the tables in conference or afterwards on more casual walks through the grounds. And the direct telephone link with London, which Churchill had installed there as soon as he first went to Chequers as Prime Minister, put many of these decisions into instant effect. 'Action this day' stimulated every bit as much scurrying about at Chequers as it did in the government departments in London.

No. 10, Downing Street and his own home at Chartwell in Kent were more in the direct range of German air attack than Buckinghamshire, and Churchill and his family used Chequers almost as a wartime home. Of course it was not inherently safer than anywhere else, and measures were taken to protect it[1] Occasionally he stayed elsewhere, such as at Ditchley in Oxfordshire over weekends when the moon was full.

At Chequers Churchill instituted the same routine as he had at Downing Street. Those on duty seldom got to bed before 3 a.m., writes Gilbert Jenkins. True, they could watch a film in the Long Gallery most weekends. For his senior staff, military and civilian, the evening routine, according to Sir Ian Jacob, was dinner which rarely finished before 10 p.m., a film and then discussions that could go on almost to dawn.

Churchill worked on several of his most important war speeches at Chequers, generally in the Hawtrey Room. Usually he had some days in which to prepare and polish them, but towards the end of June 1941 Hitler's sudden invasion of Soviet Russia left him barely a day to weigh up the consequences of coming to the support of the Russians and then putting across the decision to the British people and the rest of the world. Sir John Colville, his secretary, records thus: 'During dinner Mr Churchill said that a German

1 Churchill records a Minute from himself to the Secretary of State for Air, of 10th November 1940, in which he asks him not to send Bofors guns to Chequers. 'I cannot bear to divert Bofors from the fighting positions. What about trying a few rockets, which are at present only in an experimental stage?' But in fact the guns were sent.
The Second World War, Vol. II. Cassell, 1949.

Sir Winston Churchill, KG OM CH (1874–1965), Prime Minister, 1940–5, 1951–5, on his 80th birthday, 1954.

attack on Russia was now certain, and he thought that Hitler was counting on enlisting capitalist and right wing sympathies in this country and the USA. After dinner when I was walking on the croquet lawn with Mr Churchill, he reverted to this theme and I asked whether for him, the arch anti-Communist, this was not bowing down in the House of Rimmon. Mr Churchill replied, ''Not at all. I have only one purpose, the destruction of Hitler, and my life is much simplified thereby. If Hitler invaded Hell, I would make at least a favourable reference to the Devil in the House of Commons.'' I was awoken at 4 a.m. the following morning by a telephone message from the Foreign Office to the effect that Germany had attacked Russia. The P.M. had always said he was never to be woken up for anything but Invasion. I therefore postponed telling him till 8 a.m. His only comment was, ''Tell the BBC I will broadcast at 9 tonight.'' He began to prepare the speech at 11 a.m. and . . . devoted the whole day to it.'

Among all the people who came to Chequers during the war, many of them on numerous occasions, and including Harry Hopkins, President Roosevelt's personal representative, Dr Gilbert Winant, US Ambassador, General Eisenhower, General de Gaulle, Field Marshal Smuts and the British service chiefs and government ministers and officials, perhaps the oddest party was the Soviet delegation which came in the spring of 1942, led by Molotov, the Russian Foreign Secretary. None of the delegates would enter the house until Molotov had given his permission. At breakfast the secretaries came down first, but if Molotov appeared before they had finished, they dropped their spoons and rushed for the door. This never happened at other meals. The head housemaid, meanwhile, was startled to find a loaded revolver in Molotov's bedroom. Worse, when one evening she had to go to Molotov's room to let him know that he had not drawn his curtains and the lights were shining outside, she was greeted at the door by the Russian Foreign Secretary brandishing his gun.

Churchill's 'Caretaker' government of 1945 was defeated that summer, and when he left Chequers he wrote in the Visitors' Book one word – Finis. He was followed by Clement Attlee at the head of a Labour government. Attlee and his family took instantly to Chequers as their weekend home. He went there frequently throughout the next six years and often filled the house with guests. One, Hugh Dalton, Chancellor of the Exchequer until he made the fatal slip of 'leaking' a bit of the Budget, found it overpowering – an odd reaction from one whom Harold Macmillan described as a rollicking, jovial extrovert. In his autobiography, Attlee recorded that the family's affection for Chequers led them to retire to that part of Buckinghamshire when he left office in 1951. They bought Cherry Cottage at Prestwood, only six miles away, and when a few years later Attlee accepted an earldom, his heir's title was Viscount Prestwood.

Winston Churchill returned to power in 1951 but this time his stays at Chequers were not frequent. During the years of opposition, when he was writing his monumental history of the Second World War which deservedly won a Nobel Prize, he had grown unbreakably attached to his own country home, Chartwell, near Westerham in Kent. Its atmosphere, its facilities for entertaining and working, its environment and its distance from London were all comparable with those of Chequers, and to him much more natural. Yet, when he had a stroke in June 1953, it was to Chequers that he repaired to convalesce, towards the end of July, and he stayed there for two weeks. And his doctor, Lord Moran, found him greatly improved after the first few days there.

Churchill resigned in 1955 and was followed by Anthony Eden (later the Earl of Avon). Eden had known Chequers since the 1920s, and he had gone there often in the later 1930s when he was Foreign Secretary. In his autobiography, *Facing the Dictators*, Eden recorded how, on a visit to Chequers to see Neville Chamberlain, in 1938, at a time when they were at odds, he found the Prime Minister 'unaffected by the gulf between us'. Years later, when he was the official tenant he discovered there a 'charming and erudite' memoir on the trees in the park, written by Chamberlain.

Eden also turned to Chequers for relief and rest after the stress of political warfare which, at the time of the Suez Crisis of 1956, had been exceptionally violent. Early in 1957 he resigned and Harold Macmillan succeeded him.

Macmillan was another Prime Minister who had his own country residence[1] not very far from London, where of course he felt more at home, where things were geared for him to work, hold meetings and relax, all in the same environment. But he did use Chequers for a variety of visits and occasions, official and private. The two most significant guests were President Eisenhower, in August 1959, and the West German Chancellor, Konrad Adenauer, three months later. If there is anything symbolic in these visits, it may be in the old adage that time heals all things.

Macmillan resigned in 1963 and the Conservatives chose the Earl of Home to lead them. He surrendered his peerage and fought and won a seat in the Commons in a by-election, becoming Prime Minister as Sir Alec Douglas-Home. Chequers was not new to him; he had stayed there often in Macmillan's time when he was foreign secretary. The Conservatives were defeated by Labour in 1964 by the narrowest of margins and Harold Wilson (now Sir Harold Wilson) became Prime Minister. Since his arrival at Chequers as Prime Minister for the first term, the house has seen much more governmental activity than ever before. Sometimes it has bid fair to equal the importance of No. 10 Downing Street. Full Cabinets have been held at Chequers, the frequency and the status of visits by foreign heads of state have grown, and the volume of business done at weekends has been such that Wilson has said, in retrospect, he scarcely had time, in either of his terms, to 'go for a walk round the rose garden or swim in the pool.' Edward Heath, Prime Minister from 1970 to 1974, had much the same experience, though he has recorded in his book about music[2] that he found time to practise at the piano in the Great Hall.

1 Birch Grove, near Haywards Heath, Sussex.

2 *Music: a Joy for Life*. Sidgwick and Jackson, 1976.

The present Prime Minister, James Callaghan, and his wife and family use Chequers regularly and enjoy its relaxing atmosphere. It was from the house that Mr Callaghan, in the New Year of 1977, called upon the nation, in a broadcast, to join together to get over its economic difficulties.

Each of the Prime Ministers has used Chequers according to his individual needs and tastes, but there is one feeling that they have all had about it, namely, that it is a real home. They have been able to rest and regenerate themselves there just as they would in their own homes. To that extent Chequers has fulfilled the rôle Lord Lee intended for it.

In the window in the ante-room to the Great Parlour are set two panels of stained glass with the arms of Lord and Lady Lee, monograms AR and RA, with the inscription underneath.

Index

Printed in England for Her Majestys Stationery Office by
The Curwen Press Ltd, Plaistow, London Dd 496347 K80